RICH IN CHRIST
A Dead Dog at the King's Table

Rejoicing in, Applying, and Memorizing
up to 105 Spiritual Riches
that will Totally Change Your Life

Written by Jack Teeple

Illustrated by Joe Nuthals

Copyright © 2005

Rich in Christ Publications

"Satisfy us in the morning
with your unfailing love,
that we may sing for joy
and be glad all our days."

(Psalm 90:14)

ACKNOWLEDGMENTS

I want to thank my former pastors and Bible teachers who grounded me in Biblical truth, and the assurance that is found in Jesus Christ.

Thanks to my loving and insightful wife Pati, whose tireless help, input, and encouragement on this project was invaluable.

Thanks also to my parents, who provided me with a godly home and upbringing, my wonderful sons who bring me endless joy, and to countless Christian friends who have inspired and encouraged me all along the way.

Special thanks to Jack Lannom, who first taught me the potential of positive, Biblical thinking, and to Dawn Murbach and Connie Miller who put time and effort into making this book possible.

Above all else, my praise and worship to God, from whom all blessings flow, and to my Savior and Lord Jesus Christ who, "though he was rich, yet for your sakes he became poor, so that you through his poverty might become rich" (II Corinthians 8:9).

"For you know the grace of our Lord Jesus Christ, that though he was rich, yet for your sakes he became poor, so that you through his poverty might become rich."

(II Corinthians 8:9)

Dedicated to
The Persecuted Church

"...sorrowful, yet always rejoicing;
poor, yet making many rich;
having nothing, and yet possessing
all things."

(II Corinthians 6:10) KJV

Contents

FORWARD

What does it mean to be truly rich in Christ? To think about the wonderful blessings given to us by a holy, eternal, all-powerful God is absolutely mind boggling. Yet, astoundingly, Scripture says that I am eternally rich in Him. I don't fully understand it, but by faith I accept it as true.

As a professional athlete and running back in the NFL, my performance soared when I began to see myself as a top-level athlete. I was in the NFL, on the team and even a starter - my National Football League identity was complete. The power of such an identity, however, was only evidenced when my mind accepted and dwelt on who I was as an athlete. The more I understood that truth, the more I could then free the inbred gifts and abilities given to me as an NFL caliber performer, and work to be all that my talents would allow. It was what my mind knew and believed about the truth that made the difference in my play.

The Bible says that if you are in Christ, you are spiritually rich in Him. You have a position that includes righteousness, forgiveness, and peace with God. You are a child of God and an heir of God. It is your identity, given to you by the grace of God. Still, until you know, understand, and dwell on these aspects revealed in Scripture, you will live as if dead, and in spiritual poverty, not fully experiencing the abundance of life in Him.

My coach at Notre Dame, Lou Holtz, would say that winning is simple, but not easy. If you block and tackle better than your opponent, then you will win - simple, but not easy. Having our minds saturated with, and settled on Christ is simple to understand, but not easy to really live out, in this age of distractions and busyness.

In my estimation, God has given Jack Teeple a tool that makes living in Christ a little easier. *Rich in Christ* is an incredibly simple and awesomely profound way to hide God's Word in your heart. It is filled with Scriptures that describe who you are in Him and who He is in you. You will find, as I have, that the reality of abundant life will overflow in you as you learn what it means to be rich in Christ - as you meditate on, memorize and apply the truths in this book. *Rich in Christ* trains your mind in the Scriptures to truly know Christ, and experience His life and His fullness in you.

Anthony Johnson

Anthony Johnson played college football at the University of Notre Dame, scoring 36 touchdowns and leading the Fighting Irish to a national championship in 1988. He then went on to a successful professional career, playing for the Indianapolis Colts, New York Jets, Chicago Bears, Carolina Panthers, and Jacksonville Jaguars. Anthony currently lives with his family in Florida, where he works with the Athletes in Action ministry of Campus Crusade, and is the chaplain for the Jacksonville Jaguars.

"In whom we have redemption through his blood, the forgiveness of sins, according to the riches of his grace."

(Ephesians 1:7) KJV

Introduction

First of all, this book is to some degree a survival manual. And I will freely admit, I need it and you need it, desperately!

It's tough down here, brutal, trying to live a victorious Christian life in a fallen world, on Satan's turf. The Apostle John wrote, "The whole world is under the control of the evil one" (I John 5:19b). The Apostle Paul wrote, "For our struggle is not against flesh and blood, but against the rulers, against the authorities, against the powers of this dark world, and against the spiritual forces of evil in the heavenly realms" (Ephesians 6:12).

There is a *vicious* battle raging. The enemy is out to discourage you, disillusion you, devastate you, and if possible, destroy you. The Apostle Peter wrote, "Be self-controlled and alert. Your enemy the devil prowls around like a roaring lion looking for someone to devour" (I Peter 5:8).

The enemy is ferocious and relentless. The devil and his forces wage a fierce battle. And without a doubt, the main battlefield is your mind.

Satan and his forces don't jump out of the shadows and hit you over the head with a club. They do, however, delight in seeing you dwell in defeat, negativism, and spiritual bankruptcy, and to never live up to your glorious calling.

So let's face it, each of us desperately needs God's power to live *victoriously,* to win the day by day battles of the mind, to live in spiritual richness, not poverty.

The truths in this book will equip you to see yourself as God sees you, to understand the wonderful fact that "God's divine power has given us everything we need for life and godliness" (II Peter 1:3). Consistent victory is both accessible and attainable.

Way too often we're like the boxer in the ring getting hammered by the other guy. We're tired, and our hands are down at our sides. We're not blocking the fierce punches of the opponent, and we're paying the price. Our trainer in our corner is yelling, "Get your gloves up! Get your gloves up!" And unless we do, it's not going to be pretty.

This study is intended to help you "get your gloves up." Not only that, but it is designed to give you *victory* over your adversary, to see *him* pummeled into submission, and to learn the reality of "resisting the devil, and he will flee from you" (James 4:7). Not only will the truths in this book help you *survive*, but you'll be equipped to *thrive*, to live in daily victory.

When you have completed this study, by the simple use of the alphabet and "memory pegs" you will be able to recite in order, over 50 unchangeable, irrefutable, undeniable riches you have in Christ (or over 100 for the ambitious). These are Biblical truths and riches that you currently possess as a Christian, you will always possess, and cannot be taken away from you.

By going over this list on a regular basis, not only will it help you remember these truths, but also it will help you transform your thinking, and consistently win the battle of the mind.

By meditating on the riches you have in Christ, you will replace poor, pathetic, defeated thinking with rich, victorious thinking. This, in turn, will affect literally every area of your life.

Remember, and this is so very important, when the devil came against Jesus with lies and half-truths,

Jesus always responded with the truth of Scripture (Matthew 4:1-11). It's the same with you and me. Satan is the father of lies (John 8:44), so we must defeat him with the truth. Get ready, then, for an exciting journey, a transforming adventure. May you never be the same!

"I have written...to stimulate you to wholesome thinking."
(II Peter 3:1)

"So I tell you this, and insist on it in the Lord, that you must no longer live as the Gentiles do, in the futility of their thinking."
(Ephesians 4:17)

That's right, wholesome, victorious thinking can be yours. No more room for futile, empty thinking. I'll meet you at the King's table.

"I pray also that the eyes of your heart may be enlightened in order that you may know the hope to which he has called you, the riches of his glorious inheritance in the saints, and his incomparably great power for us who believe."

(Ephesians 1:18–19a)

Chapter 1

Always at the King's Table

There is a wonderful story in the Old Testament which reminds me so much of God's grace to all who put their faith in Jesus Christ as Savior and Lord. The passage speaks so beautifully of the riches given to us in Christ, although we are totally unworthy of such riches. The story concerns a young man named Mephibosheth, and is found in II Samuel 9.

In the story, the warrior David had been made King of Israel, and the former kingdom of Saul was no more. David asked of his officials, "Is there anyone who is left of the house of Saul, that I may show him kindness for Jonathan's sake?" (Ch. 9, vs. 1) NKJV. Jonathan was David's best friend and Saul's son, and both Jonathan and Saul had been killed in battle.

The response to David's question was this: "There is still a son of Jonathan; he is crippled in both feet" (Ch. 9, vs. 3). And so David called for this crippled son of Jonathan, whose name was Mephibosheth, and he was brought to the mighty King of Israel.

As Mephibosheth bowed before David, the king made some amazing statements. "'Don't be afraid,' David said to him, 'for I will surely show you kindness for the sake of your father Jonathan. I will restore to you all the land that belonged to your grandfather Saul, and you will always eat at my table'" (Ch. 9, vs. 7).

Now it is very noteworthy that the statement was made four times in this brief chapter of Scripture, that Mephibosheth would be allowed to "always eat at the king's table." Other wonderful promises were also given to him, but it was stressed repeatedly that Mephibosheth would eat at the king's table, just like one of the king's sons.

Mephibosheth's response to such kindness was also fascinating. "Mephibosheth bowed down and said, 'What is your servant, that you should notice a dead dog like me?'" (Ch. 9, vs. 8).

What a great picture of God's grace to us! Just as Mephibosheth could have easily been the recipient of the king's anger and judgment, instead he received an abundance of King David's mercy, grace, and riches. This "dead dog" would always eat at the king's table.

Similarly, although we deserve the judgment and punishment of God, we instead are given his mercy, grace, and riches through faith in Jesus Christ. We, like Mephibosheth, "will always eat at the king's table," but in our case we will dine at the table of the King of all kings and Lord of all lords. Think about that! Soak it in. For now and for all eternity, God has graciously chosen to lavish upon us his glorious riches in Christ, seating us at His table as His sons and daughters!

Perhaps your response, like Mephibosheth's, is

a humble, "what is your servant, that you should notice a dead dog like me?" (Actually, Mephibosheth was expressing his feelings of total worthlessness and unworthiness). But then as we, as believers in Christ, "dine at the King's table," may we also respond with profound gratitude, obedience, worship, and victorious living.

That is what this book is all about. In the following pages you will learn how to "have the mind of Christ" (I Corinthians 2:16b) NKJV. You will learn what it means to have victory in your thinking. You will be given the tools to memorize over 100 riches in Christ, unchangeable, irrefutable, undeniable riches given to us when we humble ourselves before God, and receive Jesus Christ by faith as our Savior and Lord.

And in recognizing and applying these wonderful truths and riches, you will be challenged to live a life of obedience and service to Christ, rejoicing in the spiritual riches you possess, and excited to "share the wealth" with others, inviting them also, to dine at the King's glorious table of eternal riches.*

*To make *certain* that *your* reservation has been confirmed to dine at the King's table, see page 155.

"As for you, you were dead in your transgressions and sins."

(Ephesians 2:1)

"God raised us up with Christ and seated us with him in the heavenly realms in Christ Jesus, in order that in the coming ages he might show the incomparable riches of his grace, expressed in his kindness to us in Christ Jesus."

(Ephesians 2:6-7)

Chapter 2

Riches to Wage a War and Win a War

If you've been a Christian for any length of time at all, and your desire is to truly live a victorious Christian life, you've quickly come to realize that every single day of your life you're involved in spiritual warfare. You're tempted to give in to discouragement, defeat, or despair (or all of the above). You can easily relate to the question asked in Psalm 13:2, "How long must I wrestle with my thoughts?" And you realize, in reality, that the wrestling match will continue until you're finally home in Heaven.

Consider the following Scripture:

"For though we live in the world, we do not wage war as the world does. The weapons we fight with are not the weapons of the world. On the contrary, they have divine power to demolish strongholds. We demolish arguments and every pretension that sets itself up against the knowledge of God, and we take every thought captive and make it obedient to Christ" (II Corinthians 10:3-5).

"Wage war, weapons, fight, demolish, take captive." Strong military terms. We *are* in a war, a constant battle for our minds. We *must* conform our thinking to Scripture to be victorious on a consistent basis. Too many Christians accept and cling to an ongoing defeatist "dead dog" mindset, rather than rejoicing in and responding to their glorious riches in Christ.

But the fact is, and as Scripture clearly teaches, we have been given great power through the Holy Spirit and the Word of God to live in victorious thinking, which naturally leads to victorious living. It's time to be set free from the negativism, pessimism, and fatalism that tend to dominate our thoughts.

Think about it! When we as Christians are characterized by gloominess and complaining, rather than the joy and peace that should daily flow from each of us due to our position and richness in Christ, is it any wonder that the world isn't attracted to the Savior? As you will soon see, Christians always have something to rejoice about and be thankful for. It's time to start thinking right!

"Finally, brethren, whatever things are true, whatever things are honest, whatever things are just, whatever things are pure, whatever things are lovely, whatever things are of good report; if there be any virtue, and if any praise, think on these things" (Philippians 4:8) KJV.

"Blessed is the man who walks not in the counsel of the ungodly, nor stands in the path of sinners, nor sits in the seat of the scornful; but his delight is in the law of the LORD, and on his law he meditates day and night" (Psalm 1:1-2) NKJV.

"Let this mind be in you, which was also in Christ Jesus" (Philippians 2:5) KJV.

"We have the mind of Christ" (I Corinthians 2:16b) KJV.

"And be not conformed to this world, but be transformed by the renewing of your mind" (Romans 12:2a) KJV.

"Those who live according to the sinful nature have their minds set on what that nature desires; but those who live in accordance with the Spirit have their minds set on what the Spirit desires. The mind of sinful man is death, but the mind controlled by the Spirit is life and peace" (Romans 8:5-6).

Your life is made up largely of the choices you make, and the opportunity is here and now to make right choices in your thinking and attitude. With a right and Biblical attitude, joy and peace become a reality as well. Proverbs 15:15 says, "All the days of the oppressed are wretched, but the cheerful heart has a continual feast." Let's leave the "wretched" behind. God has something infinitely better for us. Let's join Mephibosheth in a rich feast at the King's table.

"Why spend money on what is not bread, and your labor on what does not satisfy? Listen, listen to me, and eat what is good, and your soul will delight in the richest of fare."

(Isaiah 55:2)

Chapter 3

Riches in Christ (Alphabetical)

Some time ago I spoke at a wonderful inner city church called "Love Church" in Fort Wayne, Indiana. The people there are not very well off financially, to say the very least. I began my message, therefore, by informing them that I had heard that some of the richest people in Fort Wayne attended their church. In fact, I told them I knew that some of the richest people in the *world* attended Love Church. Well, by that time I had their attention. It wasn't long before they understood that I was speaking to them about spiritual riches, and they were rejoicing enthusiastically about the riches they possessed. As they left for home that evening, their minds were joyously *filled* with dozens of riches in Christ, all given by His grace.

So now let's talk ABC's. In this chapter you will see some wonderful truths and riches in Christ, and how to commit them to memory by using the alphabet. When it comes to memorizing riches in Christ alphabetically, you can keep it pretty simple, or you can take the challenge to go deeper and memorize multiple riches per each letter. I suggest keeping it simple at first. Here's how:

Each one of the riches listed alphabetically focuses on a key word. For example: Under **A**, "**A**ll my sins are forgiven." The key word is "**A**ll", and it starts with "A". "**A**ll my sins are forgiven."

Under **B** , "I am **B**ought with a price, the **B**lood of Christ." The key words are "**B**ought" and "**B**lood," both starting with the letter "B."

This will work with all of the riches from A to Z. Each one will have a "trigger word" starting with that letter of the alphabet. After you've learned one of the riches for each letter of the alphabet, and you want to add more riches to your list, most of the letters of the alphabet have additional riches to memorize. So have fun. And you'll find that it's easier to memorize God's truth than you've ever imagined.

Not only that, but the more riches you hide in your heart and mind, the more you'll find your thinking being transformed on a regular basis into "the mind of Christ."

I know a number of people who think about and rejoice in their riches in Christ before they go to sleep at night. They share how God's truth provides peace and comfort, and a good night's rest. Replacing worry and anxiety with the rich promises of God does indeed provide a "peace that transcends all understanding" (Philippians 4:7).

Now, on to letter A, and the beginning of our riches in Christ!

<u>A</u>ll my sins are forgiven.

"...who forgives all your sins, and heals
all your diseases."   (Psalm 103:3)

"He forgave us all our sins."
(Colossians 2:13b)

I can do <u>A</u>ll things through Christ who strengthens me.

"I can do all things through Christ
who strengthens me."
(Philippians 4:13) KJV

God is <u>A</u>ble to save me completely.

"Therefore he is able to save completely
those who come to God through him,
because he always lives to intercede for
them." (Hebrews 7:25)

I am **B**ought with a price, the **B**lood of Christ.

"You were bought at a price.
Therefore honor God with your body."
(1 Corinthians 6:20)

"… the church of God,
which he has purchased with his own blood."
(Acts 20:28b) KJV

I am **B**orn from above. (**B**orn again)

"In reply Jesus declared, 'I tell you the truth,
no one can see the kingdom of God
unless he is born again.'"
(John 3:3)

I will have a **B**rand-new **B**ody.

"So will it be with the resurrection of the dead.
The body that is sown is perishable,
it is raised imperishable;
it is sown in dishonor,
it is raised in glory;
it is sown in weakness,
it is raised in power;
it is sown a natural body,
it is raised a spiritual body.
If there is a natural body,
there is also a spiritual body."
(I Corinthians 15:42-44)

"...he will transform our lowly bodies so that
they will be like his glorious body."
(Philippians 3:21b)

I am <u>C</u>omplete in <u>C</u>hrist.

"You are complete in Him."
(Colossians 2:10) KJV

I am <u>C</u>reated in <u>C</u>hrist to do good works.

"For we are God's workmanship, created in Christ Jesus to do good works, which God prepared in advance for us to do."
(Ephesians 2:10)

I can <u>C</u>ast all my <u>C</u>ares upon Him because He <u>C</u>ares for me.

"Casting all your care upon on him for he cares for you."
(I Peter 5:7) NKJV

I am **D**elivered from the **D**ominion of **D**arkness.

"For he has rescued us from the dominion of darkness and brought us into the kingdom of the Son he loves, in whom we have redemption, the forgiveness of sins."
(Colossians 1:13-14)

I have **D**irect access into the presence of God.

"Therefore, brothers, since we have confidence to enter the Most Holy Place by the blood of Jesus, by a new and living way opened for us through the curtain, that is, his body, and since we have a great priest over the house of God, let us draw near to God with a sincere heart in full assurance of faith, having our hearts sprinkled to cleanse us from a guilty conscience and having our bodies washed with pure water."   (Hebrews 10:19-22)

I have __E__ternal life.

"For God so loved the world that he gave his one
and only Son, that whoever believes in him shall
not perish but have eternal life."
(John 3:16)

"I tell you the truth, whoever hears my word
and believes him who sent me
has eternal life and will not be condemned;
he has crossed over from death to life."
(John 5:24)

As far as the __E__ast is from the west, so has God taken my sins from me.

"As far as the east is from the west, so far has He
removed our transgressions from us."
(Psalm 103:12) NKJV

God is my __F__aithful __F__ather.

"Grace to you, and peace, from God our Father,
and the Lord Jesus Christ."
(Ephesians 1:2) KJV

"For the word of the LORD is right and true;
he is faithful in all he does."
(Psalm 33:4)

I am __F__ree in Christ.

"It is for freedom that Christ has set us free.
Stand firm, then, and do not let yourselves be
burdened again by a yoke of slavery."
(Galatians 5:1)

"You, my brothers, were called to be free. But do
not use your freedom to indulge the sinful nature;
rather, serve one another in love."
(Galatians 5:13)

I have been **G**iven
the **G**ift of **G**race.

"For it is by grace you have been saved,
through faith - and this not from
yourselves, it is the gift of God - not by works,
so that no one can boast."
(Ephesians 2:8-9)

Every day is a **G**ift from **G**od.

"This is the day the LORD has made;
we will rejoice and be glad in it."
(Psalm 118:24) NKJV

"The God who made the world and everything
in it is the Lord of heaven and earth and does
not live in temples built by hands. And he is
not served by human hands, as if he needed
anything, because he himself gives all men life
and breath and everything else."
(Acts 17:24-25)

<u>H</u>eaven is my <u>H</u>ome.

"But our citizenship is in heaven. And we
eagerly await a Savior from there, the Lord
Jesus Christ, who, by the power that enables
him to bring everything under his control,
will transform our lowly bodies so that
they will be like his glorious body."
(Philippians 3:20-21)

My <u>H</u>ope is an anchor.

"We have this hope as an anchor for the soul,
firm and secure." (Hebrews 6:19a)

The <u>H</u>oly Spirit is in me.

"Do you not know that your body is a temple
of the Holy Spirit, who is in you, whom you
have received from God?"
(I Corinthians 6:19)

With God nothing is Impossible.

"For with God nothing will be impossible."
(Luke 1:37) NKJV

God's gifts are Irrevocable.

"For God's gifts and his call are irrevocable."
(Romans 11:29)

<u>J</u>esus is my best friend.

"… there is a friend who sticks closer
than a brother."
(Proverbs 18:24b) NKJV

<u>J</u>esus is my Savior.

"We have put our hope in the living God,
who is the Savior of all men,
and especially of those who believe."
(I Timothy 4:10)

"Today in the town of David a Savior has been
born to you; he is Christ the Lord."
(Luke 2:11)

<u>J</u>esus is my Lord.

"and that every tongue should confess that
Jesus Christ is Lord, to the glory of
God the Father." (Philippians 2:11) NKJV

Jesus is coming back soon for me.

"'Men of Galilee,' they said, 'why do you stand here looking into the sky? This same Jesus, who has been taken from you into heaven, will come back in the same way you have seen him go into heaven.'"
(Acts 1:11)

"Let not your heart be troubled;
you believe in God, believe also in Me.
In My Father's house are many mansions;
if it were not so, I would have told you.
I go to prepare a place for you.
And if I go and prepare a place for you,
I will come again and receive you to Myself;
that where I am, there you may be also."
(John 14:1-3) NKJV

I am a child of the **K**ing.

"The Lord will rescue me from every evil attack and will bring me safely to his heavenly kingdom." (II Timothy 4:18a)

"Therefore, since we are receiving a kingdom that cannot be shaken, let us be thankful, and so worship God acceptably with reverence and awe." (Hebrews 12:28)

I **K**now I have eternal life.

"These things I have written to you who believe in the name of the Son of God, that you may know that you have eternal life." (1 John 5:13a) NKJV

"Now we know that if the earthly tent we live in is destroyed, we have a building from God, an eternal house in heaven, not built by human hands." (II Corinthians 5:1)

I **K**now God.
God **K**nows me.

"Formerly, when you did not know God,
you were slaves to those who by nature
are not gods. But now that you know
God - or rather are known by God - how is it
that you are turning back to those weak and
miserable principles? Do you wish to be
enslaved by them all over again?"
(Galatians 4:8-9)

"I am the good shepherd; and I know My
sheep, and am known by My own. As the
Father knows Me, even so I know the Father;
and I lay down My life for the sheep."
(John 10:14-15) NKJV

Nothing can separate me from God's **L**ove.

"For I am convinced that neither death nor life, neither angels nor demons, neither the present nor the future, nor any powers, neither height nor depth, nor anything else in all creation, will be able to separate us from the love of God that is in Christ Jesus our Lord."
(Romans 8:38-39)

Because He **L**ives, I too shall **L**ive.

"I will not leave you orphans; I will come to you. A little while longer and the world will see Me no more, but you will see Me. Because I live, you will live also."
(John 14:18-19) NKJV

I am **M**ade in the image of God.

"Then God said, 'Let Us make man in Our image, according to Our likeness,'... So God created man in His own image, in the image of God He created him; male and female He created them." (Genesis 1:26-27) NKJV

I have received God's **M**ercy.

"Praise be to the God and Father of our Lord Jesus Christ! In his great mercy he has given us new birth into a living hope through the resurrection of Jesus Christ from the dead." (I Peter 1:3)

I have the **M**ind of Christ.

"But we have the mind of Christ." (I Corinthians 2:16b) KJV

Never, Never, Never will God leave me or forsake me.

"...God has said, 'Never will I leave you; never will I forsake you.' So we say with confidence, 'The Lord is my helper; I will not be afraid. What can man do to me?'" (Hebrews 13:5b-6)

My sins are Nailed to the cross.

"When you were dead in your sins and in the uncircumcision of your sinful nature, God made you alive with Christ. He forgave us all our sins, having canceled the written code, with its regulations, that was against us and that stood opposed to us; he took it away, nailing it to the cross. And having disarmed the powers and authorities, he made a public spectacle of them, triumphing over them by the cross." (Colossians 2:13-15)

God will meet all my <u>N</u>eeds.

"Therefore I tell you,
do not worry about your life,
what you will eat or drink;
or about your body, what you will wear.
Is not life more important than food,
and the body more important than clothes?
Look at the birds of the air;
they do not sow or reap or store away in barns,
and yet your Heavenly Father feeds them. Are
you not much more valuable than they?
Who of you by worrying can add a
single hour to his life?"
(Matthew 6:25-27)

"And my God shall supply all your need
according to His riches in glory by
Christ Jesus."
(Philippians 4:19) NKJV

God **O**wns me.

"Now it is God who makes both us and you stand firm in Christ. He anointed us, set his seal of ownership on us, and put his Spirit in our hearts as a deposit, guaranteeing what is to come."   (II Corinthians 1:21-22)

I can **O**pen my mouth wide and God will fill it.

"Open thy mouth wide, and I will fill it." (Psalm 81:10) KJV

I am an **O**vercomer.

"Who is he who overcomes the world, but he who believes that Jesus is the Son of God?" (I John 5:5)

I have **P**eace with God.

"Therefore being justified by faith,
we have peace with God through our
Lord Jesus Christ." (Romans 5:1) KJV

I am **P**erfect in His sight.

"...because by one sacrifice he has made
perfect forever those who are being made
holy." (Hebrews 10:14)

My life has great **P**urpose.

"… by his power he may fulfill every good
purpose of yours and every act prompted by
your faith." (II Thessalonians 1:11b)

"'For I know the plans I have for you,'
declares the LORD, 'plans to prosper you and
not to harm you, plans to give you
hope and a future.'"
(Jeremiah 29:11)

My life has great **Q**uality.

"For no one can lay any foundation other than the one already laid, which is Jesus Christ. If any man builds on this foundation using gold, silver, costly stones, wood, hay or straw, his work will be shown for what it is, because the Day will bring it to light. It will be revealed with fire, and the fire will test the quality of each man's work." (I Corinthians 3:11-13)

"...whosoever desires to become great among you, let him be your servant. And whoever desires to be first among you, let him be your slave - just as the Son of Man did not come to be served, but to serve, and to give His life a ransom for many." (Matthew 20:26b-28)

"Those who are wise will shine like the brightness of the heavens, and those who lead many to righteousness, like the stars for ever and ever." (Daniel 12:3)

I've been **R**edeemed by the blood of the Lamb.

"For you know that it was not with perishable things such as silver or gold that you were redeemed from the empty way of life handed down to you from your forefathers, but with the precious blood of Christ, a lamb without blemish or defect." (I Peter 1:18-19)

I am **R**aised with Christ.

"… but God has raised us up together, and made us sit together in heavenly places in Christ Jesus." (Ephesians 2:6) KJV

God is my **R**efuge and strength.

"God is our refuge and strength, a very present help in trouble. Therefore we will not fear, though the earth be removed, and though the mountains be carried into the midst of the sea." (Psalm 46:1-2) KJV

I am <u>S</u>ecure in Christ.

"And I give them eternal life, and they shall never perish; neither shall anyone snatch them out of My hand. My Father, who has given them to Me, is greater than all; no one is able to snatch them out of My Father's hand."
(John 10:28-29) NKJV

I am <u>S</u>ealed by the Holy <u>S</u>pirit.

"Now it is God who makes both us and you stand firm in Christ. He anointed us, set his seal of ownership on us, and put his Spirit in our hearts as a deposit, guaranteeing what is to come." (II Corinthians 1:21-22)

"And do not grieve the Holy Spirit of God, by whom you were sealed for the day of redemption." (Ephesians 4:30) NKJV

I am **S**aved.

"whoever calls on the name
of the LORD shall be saved."
(Romans 10:13) NKJV

I am **S**eated in the heavenlies.

"And God raised us up with Christ and
seated us with him in the heavenly realms
in Christ Jesus."
(Ephesians 2:6)

The Lord is my **S**hepherd.

"The Lord is my shepherd,
I shall not want."
(Psalm 23:1) KJV

I am **S**anctified. (**S**et apart)

"But you were washed, you were sanctified,
you were justified in the name of the Lord
Jesus Christ and by the Spirit of our God."
(I Corinthians 6:11b)

I've come to know the **T**ruth,
and the **T**ruth has set me free.

"To the Jews who had believed him,
Jesus said, 'If you hold to my teaching,
you are really my disciples.
Then you will know the truth,
and the truth will set you free.'"
(John 8:31-32)

I can **T**rust in the LORD
with all my heart.

"Trust in the LORD with all your heart,
and lean not on your own understanding;
in all your ways acknowledge Him,
and he shall direct your paths."
(Proverbs 3:5-6) NKJV

U

God loves me with an <u>U</u>nconditional love.

"Praise be to the God and Father of our Lord Jesus Christ, who has blessed us in the heavenly realms with every spiritual blessing in Christ. For he chose us in him before the creation of the world to be holy and blameless in his sight. In love he predestined us to be adopted as his sons through Jesus Christ, in accordance with his pleasure and will - to the praise of his glorious grace, which he has freely given us in the One he loves."
(Ephesians 1:3-6)

God loves me with an <u>U</u>nfailing love.

"Many are the woes of the wicked, but the LORD's unfailing love surrounds the man who trusts in him." (Psalm 32:10)

I have great **V**alue in Christ.

"Are not two sparrows sold for a copper coin?
And not one of them falls to the ground apart
from your Father's will. But the very hairs of
your head are all numbered. Do not fear
therefore: you are of more value
than many sparrows."
(Matthew 10:29-31) NKJV

I have great **V**ictory in Christ.

"With God we will gain the victory, and he will
trample down our enemies."
(Psalm 60:12)

"But thanks be to God, who gives us the victory
through our Lord Jesus Christ."
(I Corinthians 15:57) NKJV

I have great **W**isdom in Christ.

"If any of you lacks wisdom, he should ask
God, who gives generously to all without
finding fault, and it will be given to him."
(James 1:5)

I can **W**orship the Father
in spirit and truth.

"But the hour is coming, and now is, when the
true worshipers will worship the Father in spirit
and truth; for the Father is seeking such to
worship Him. God is Spirit, and those who
worship Him must worship in spirit and truth."
(John 4:23-24) NKJV

I am God's **W**orkmanship.

"For we are God's workmanship,
created in Christ Jesus to do good works,
which God prepared in advance for us to do."
(Ephesians 2:10)

I am a **W**itness for God.

"But you shall receive power when the
Holy Spirit has come upon you;
and you shall be witnesses to Me in
Jerusalem, and in all Judea and Samaria,
and to the end of the earth."
(Acts 1:8) NKJV

"You yourselves are our letter, written on our
hearts, known and read by everybody.
You show that you are a letter from Christ,
the result of our ministry, written not with ink
but with the Spirit of the living God,
not on tablets of stone but on tablets
of human hearts."
(II Corinthians 3:2-3)

I have an e<u>X</u>cellent life.

"But just as you excel in everything - in faith,
in speech, in knowledge, in complete
earnestness and in your love for us - see that
you also excel in this grace of giving."
(II Corinthians 8:7)

"This is a trustworthy saying.
And I want you to stress these things,
so that those who have trusted in God
may be careful to devote themselves
to doing what is good.
These things are excellent and
profitable for everyone."
(Titus 3:8)

I am **Y**oked together with Christ.

"Come to Me, all you who labor and are heavy laden, and I will give you rest. Take My yoke upon you and learn from Me, for I am gentle and lowly in heart, and you will find rest for your souls. For My yoke is easy and My burden is light." (Matthew 11:28-30) NKJV

"Jesus Christ is the same **Y**esterday, today, and forever."

"Remember your leaders, who spoke the word of God to you. Consider the outcome of their way of life and imitate their faith. Jesus Christ is the same yesterday and today and forever."
(Hebrews 13:7-8)

I have great <u>Z</u>eal for God.

"Never be lacking in zeal,
but keep your spiritual fervor,
serving the Lord."
(Romans 12:11)

"It is fine to be zealous, provided the
purpose is good."   (Galatians 4:18a)

I have come to Mt. <u>Z</u>ion.

"But you have come to Mount Zion, to the
heavenly Jerusalem, the city of the living God.
You have come to thousands upon thousands
of angels in joyful assembly, to the church of
the firstborn, whose names are written in
heaven. You have come to God, the judge of
all men, to the spirits of righteous men made
perfect." (Hebrews 12:22-23)

There they are, the spiritual riches that each true believer in Jesus Christ possesses, from A to Z.

By the way, parents, this is an excellent way to teach God's truth to your children, to help them learn and remember who they are and what they possess in Christ. It's a phenomenal way to make young disciples. (See Epilogue, p. 146).

I hope you will enjoy going through your "alphabetical riches" as much as I do. If you memorize *all* the riches listed in this chapter, you'll have 69 riches! And whether you memorize 29, 49, or 69, if you go through your list once a day, every day, you will *never* forget them!

Now here's where it gets even *more* exciting. We're going to "hang" some more riches on 26 "memory pegs", and add those to our alphabetical list. Very simple. And a whole lot of fun. Ready to use your imagination?

"He will be the sure
foundation for your
times, a rich store of
salvation and wisdom
and knowledge; the fear
of the LORD is the key
to this treasure."

(Isaiah 33:6)

Chapter 4

The Ten Memory Pegs

The following ten "memory pegs" can be used to memorize any number of different lists of items. For example, I've used them to memorize the ten plagues of Egypt, or a list of shopping items. To utilize the memory pegs, you must see each one as corresponding to a number. Visualize each one, use your imagination, and you'll find it to be fun and simple, and very practical in memorizing more riches in Christ in the next chapter.

So now you can turn the page and see how the first ten memory pegs correspond to numbers 1 through 10.

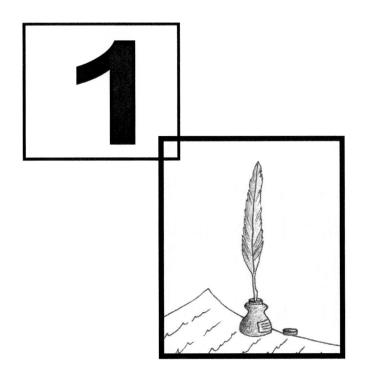

Feather

The first peg is a feather. See the feather standing straight up and down like the number 1.

Coat Hanger

The second peg is a coat hanger. See the
hanger forming the number 2.

Wheelbarrow

The third peg is a wheelbarrow. See the 3 "legs" of the wheelbarrow as representing the number 3.

Wagon

The fourth peg is a wagon. See the four-wheeled wagon as representing the number 4.

5-Dollar
Gold Piece

The fifth peg is a 5-Dollar gold piece. See the
5-Dollar gold piece as representing the
number 5.

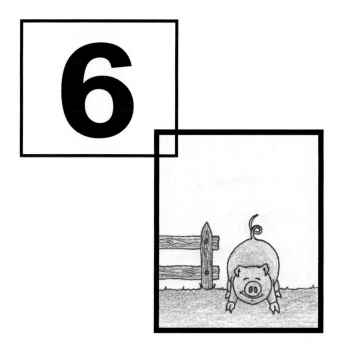

Pig's Tail

The sixth peg is a pig's tail. See the pig's
curly tail forming the number 6.

Hockey Stick

The seventh peg is an upside-down hockey
stick forming the number 7.

8

All Ate Up

The eighth peg plays on the word "ate". The bag of cookies is empty, "all ate up," because someone or something ate them all.

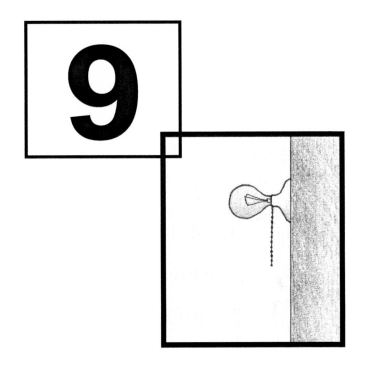

Light Bulb

The ninth peg is a light bulb pointing sideways.
See the light bulb form the number 9.

10

Ten Little Natives

The tenth peg is a group of 10 little natives.
They represent the number 10.

I encourage you to keep going over the 10 pegs until you have them memorized. It won't take long. Say them out loud. "1 is a feather. 2 is a coat hanger. 3 is a wheelbarrow." See the *number* as the *object* in your mind.

As I said, these ten pegs can be used to memorize any *number* of things. We are now going to use them, however, to memorize more wonderful riches in Christ.

"Now Joshua was dressed in filthy clothes as he stood before the angel. The angel said to those who were standing before him, 'Take off his filthy clothes'. Then he said to Joshua, 'See, I have taken away your sin, and I will put rich garments on you.'"

(Zechariah 3:3–4)

Chapter 5

More Riches in Christ
(Memory Pegs 1-10)

You are now well on your way to developing, more and more, "the mind of Christ." The more you think about, apply, and memorize the riches you have in Christ, the more joy, peace, and victory you will experience.

Like Mephibosheth, humbly and gratefully dining at King David's table, awed by the king's favor, so you will humbly and gratefully feel awed to dine at God's table of spiritual riches. So now let's add more riches that we can rejoice in and respond to, by using the 10 memory pegs.

Peg #1 is the feather. Now see the feather dipped in ink and writing *your* name in the Book of Life.

Peg #1

My name is written in the Book of Life.

"...these women who labored with me in the gospel, with Clement also, and the rest of my fellow workers, whose names are in the Book of Life."   (Philippians 4:3b) NKJV

"But you have come to Mount Zion, to the heavenly Jerusalem, the city of the living God. You have come to thousands upon thousands of angels in joyful assembly, to the church of the firstborn, whose names are written in heaven."   (Hebrews 12:22-23a)

Now see the coat hanger, peg #2. God is taking
His robe of righteousness off the hanger and
wrapping you in it.

Peg #2

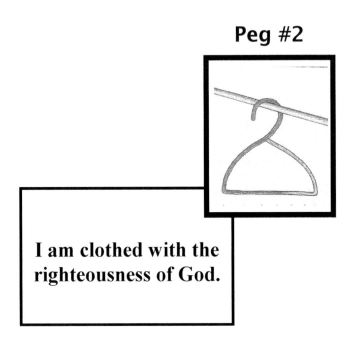

**I am clothed with the
righteousness of God.**

"I will greatly rejoice in the LORD; my soul shall
be joyful in my God; for He has clothed me with the
garments of salvation, He has covered me with the
robe of righteousness." (Isaiah 61:10a) NKJV

"God made him who had no sin to be sin for us, so
that in him we might become the righteousness of
God." (II Corinthians 5:21)

Peg #3 is the wheelbarrow. See little child pushing the wheelbarrow filled with all kinds of treasure. You are that child and the treasure is reserved for you in heaven, as an heir of God.

Peg #3

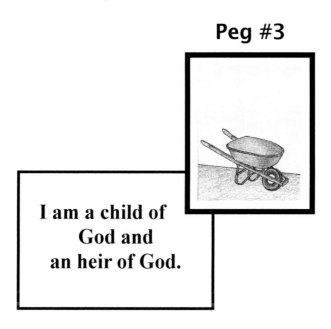

I am a child of God and an heir of God.

"Yet to all who received him, to those who believed in his name, he gave the right to become children of God." (John 1:12)

"Now if we are children, then we are heirs - heirs of God and co-heirs of Christ, if indeed we share in His sufferings in order that we may also share in His glory." (Romans 8:17)

Peg #4 is the wagon. Some big church buildings contain statues of "saints." Imagine this wagon holding a huge statue of a "saint," and the saint is you!

Peg #4

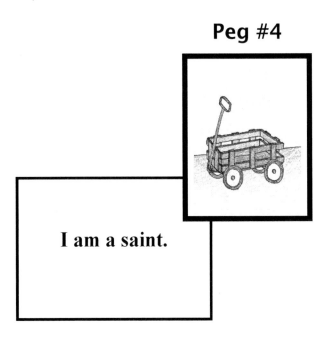

I am a saint.

"Paul, an apostle of Jesus Christ by the will of God, to the saints who are in Ephesus, and faithful in Christ Jesus: Grace to you and peace from God our Father and the Lord Jesus Christ."
(Ephesians 1:1-2) NKJV

"to all the saints in Christ Jesus at Philippi… grace and peace to you." (Philippians 1:1b-2a)

Peg #5 is the five-dollar gold piece, a symbol of your richness in Christ.

Peg #5

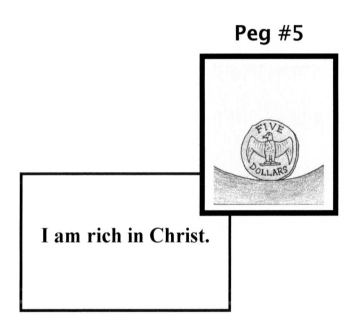

I am rich in Christ.

"...in order that in the coming ages he might show the incomparable riches of his grace, expressed in his kindness to us in Christ Jesus."
(Ephesians 2:7)

"Although I am less than the least of all God's people, this grace was given me: to preach to the Gentiles the unsearchable riches of Christ."
(Ephesians 3:8)

Peg #6 is the pig's tail. You are not pig; you are a *new* creature. And you will *remain* a new creature. God will complete His work in you.

Peg #6

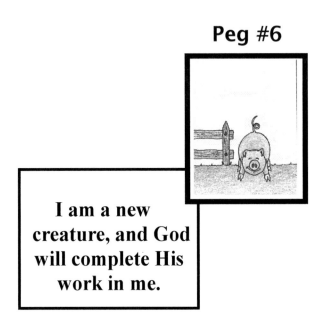

I am a new creature, and God will complete His work in me.

"Therefore, if anyone is in Christ, he is a new creation; old things have passed away; behold, all things have become new."
(II Corinthians 5:17) NKJV

"Being confident of this, that he who began a good work in you will carry it on to completion until the day of Christ Jesus." (Philippians 1:6)

The hockey stick is peg #7. You're playing street hockey with that stick, and your powerful shot at the goal knocks the goal over and about 50 yards down the street. God has filled you with His great power.

Peg #7

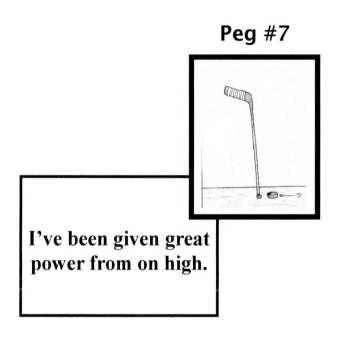

I've been given great power from on high.

"But you shall receive power when the Holy Spirit has come upon you; and you shall be witnesses to Me in Jerusalem, and in all Judea and Samaria, and to the end of the earth." (Acts 1:8) NKJV

"His divine power has given us everything we need for life and godliness through our knowledge of him who called us by his own glory and goodness." (II Peter 1:3)

Peg #8 is "all ate up." The cookies are all gone and you didn't get any. But that's okay because God has other plans, better plans for you.

Peg #8

All things work together for good to those that love God, and God makes all things beautiful in His time.

"And we know that in all things God works for the good of those who love him, who have been called according to his purpose." (Romans 8:28)

"He has made everything beautiful in its time." (Ecclesiastes 3:11a) NKJV

The light bulb is peg #9, shining brightly. It totally removes the darkness, and 3 riches hang on this peg.

Peg #9

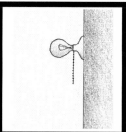

I am no longer in darkness but I am in the light. I follow Jesus, the light of the world, and I am called to be the light of the world.

"For you were once darkness, but now you are light in the Lord. Walk as children of light (for the fruit of the Spirit is in all goodness, righteousness, and truth)." (Ephesians 5:8-9) NKJV

"Then Jesus spoke to them again, saying, 'I am the light of the world. He who follows Me shall not walk in darkness, but have the light of life." (John 8:12) NKJV

"You are the light of the world. A city that is set on a hill cannot be hidden." (Matthew 5:14) NKJV

Peg #10 is 10 little natives. As you're standing among the 10 natives, God chooses you and adopts you into his family.

Peg #10

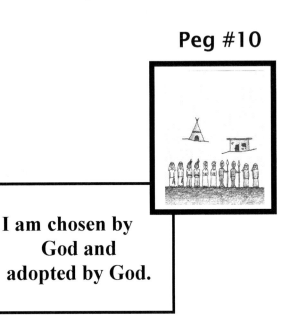

I am chosen by God and adopted by God.

"But you are a chosen people, a royal priesthood, a holy nation, a people belonging to God, that you may declare the praises of him who called you out of darkness into his wonderful light." (I Peter 2:9)

"For he chose us in Him before the creation of the world to be holy and blameless in his sight. In love he predestined us to be adopted as his sons through Jesus Christ, in accordance with his pleasure and will." (Ephesians 1:4-5)

Each of the preceding riches is based upon the blessings and promises of Almighty God. We certainly can't depend upon much in this unstable, uncertain world, but we can always depend upon God to be faithful to those whose trust is in Him.

Now, before you learn 16 more memory pegs, and more corresponding riches, it would be good to review what you've begun to learn up to this point.

Take some time to once again review your alphabetical riches. Also, take some time to visualize the first 10 pegs and really think about and thank God for the riches attached to each one. Meditate on the truths. Begin to truly see how God sees you. Let your thinking and life be powerfully and eternally transformed. When you're ready to continue, there are more exciting pegs and priceless riches to come.

"But as for me,
I will always have hope.
I will praise you more
and more."

(Psalm 71:14)

Chapter 6

Sixteen More Pegs

Are you ready? Now let's learn sixteen more memory pegs, so that you can easily memorize another sixteen items (and more) in order. Again, a vitally important *key* to successful memorization is *seeing* the number as the corresponding memory peg. The picture of each peg will easily help you do that.

Turn the page and let's continue!

Ladder

The eleventh peg is a ladder leading up to a gallows, where executions take place. See the legs of the ladder form the number 11.

12

Dozen Donuts

The twelfth peg is a dozen donuts.
When you think of the number 12,
think of 12 donuts.

13

Unlucky Thirteen

The thirteenth peg is the number 13,
unlucky 13, often associated with
bad luck and superstition.

14

Fort

The fourteenth peg is a fort.
So when you think of the number 14,
think of a fort (forteen).

Road Sign

The fifteenth peg is a fifteen mile
road marker. For example,
15 miles to heaven.

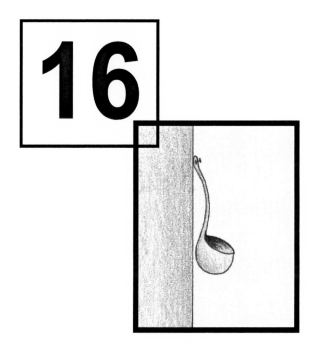

Water Ladle

The sixteenth peg is a water ladle hanging on a wall. When you think of the number 16, see a water ladle hanging on a wall.

Pocket Knife

The seventeenth peg is a partially opened pocket knife stuck in a tree. The tree and knife form the number 17.

18

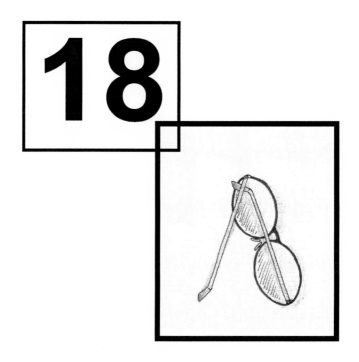

Pair of Eyeglasses

The eighteenth peg is a pair of eyeglasses. The eyeglass frames and one of the arms form the number 18.

19

Girl Holding
A Balloon

The nineteenth peg is a very thin girl holding
a balloon on a string. When you think of the
number 19, picture the thin girl and the
balloon.

20

Snake

The twentieth peg is a snake all coiled up.
You see the snake forming the number 20.

You Must Be 21

The twenty-first peg is the number 21, as in "You must be 21 to enter."

22

22 Sticks Of Dynamite

The twenty-second peg is 22 sticks of dynamite all bound together. So the number 22 will bring to mind 22 sticks of dynamite.

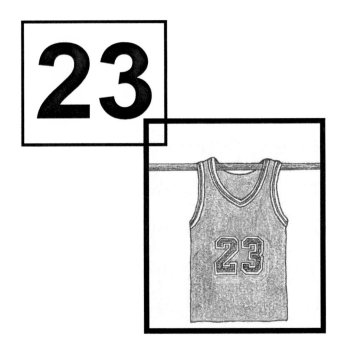

Basketball Jersey

The twenty-third peg is the number on a certain famous basketball player's jersey. Think of the number 23, and picture this jersey and this player.

24

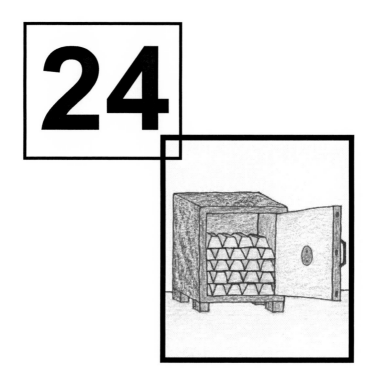

24 Gold Bars

The twenty-fourth peg is
24 gold bars in a safe.

25 Cent Piece

The twenty-fifth peg is a 25 cent piece.
Number 25 - 25 cents.

26

Ice Cream Scoop

The twenty-sixth peg is an ice cream scoop
with the emphasis on the 6 in 26.
When you hear the number 26,
think ice cream (maybe 26 flavors).

You now have twenty-six invaluable memory pegs. Practice saying all 26 pegs, in your mind, and out loud. When you add these pegs to the alphabet, as you'll see, you will soon be able to memorize, in order, up to 105 unchangeable, irrefutable, undeniable riches you have in Christ.

As I recite my list each day, I always find my thinking transformed and conformed to God's truth. Satan's assault on my thinking is met head-on and defeated.

I am in a practical and real way putting on the "armor of God" spoken of in Ephesians 6:11, so that I can effectively and victoriously "take my stand against the devil's schemes."

The devil is a liar and the father of lies (John 8:44), and he delights in discouraging, disillusioning, and deceiving us. He wants to defeat us and render us ineffective in our Christian lives, and he *doesn't* want us dwelling on *who* we are and *what* we are in Christ.

But dwell we must, and win we will. Let's now hang more priceless riches on our memory pegs.

"I rejoice at Your word as one who finds great treasure."

(Psalm 119:162) NKJV

Chapter 7

Even More Riches in Christ (Memory Pegs 11-26)

As you think about these spiritual riches in Christ, and commit them to memory, keep in mind that literally *nothing* is more important than focusing on Biblical truth. Sadly, multitudes of Christians live in perpetual discouragement and defeat, experiencing life that is both powerless and joyless, but this certainly doesn't need to be the case. God has truly provided us with all we need to live in rich spiritual victory. Now on to our memory pegs and spiritual riches.

Peg #11 is the ladder, leading up to a gallows, where executions take place, but not *your* execution. You have been declared righteous (justified), and you are accepted in Christ.

Peg #11

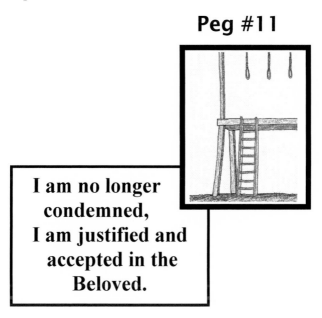

I am no longer condemned, I am justified and accepted in the Beloved.

"Therefore, there is now no condemnation for those who are in Christ Jesus." (Romans 8:1)

"Therefore, having been justified by faith, we have peace with God through our Lord Jesus Christ." (Romans 5:1) NKJV

"We are accepted in the Beloved." (Ephesians 1:6) KJV

The dozen donuts make up peg #12. Donuts have holes in the center. You are holy because of Christ.

Peg #12

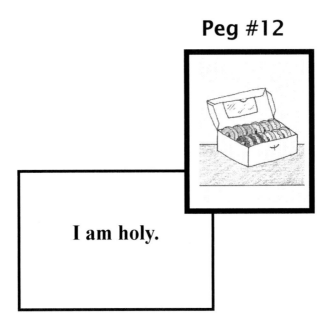

I am holy.

"Paul, an apostle of Christ Jesus by the will of God, and Timothy our brother, to the holy and faithful brothers in Christ at Colosse: Grace and peace to you from God our Father."
(Colossians 1:1-2)

Peg #13 is unlucky number 13, a superstition to some, but no worry to you, a conqueror by Christ's power.

Peg #13

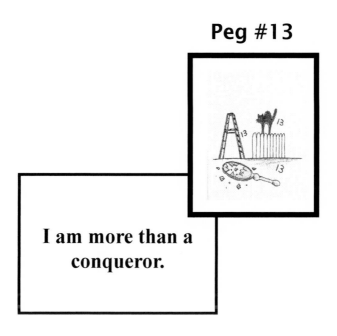

I am more than a conqueror.

"Yet in all these things we are more than conquerors through Him who loved us."
(Romans 8:37) NKJV

Peg #14 is the fort. The fort is high and thick, a stronghold for the enemy, but with God's help you can destroy it.

Peg #14

I have divine power to demolish strongholds.

"For though we live in the world, we do not wage war as the world does. The weapons we fight with are not the weapons of the world. On the contrary, they have divine power to demolish strongholds. We demolish arguments and every pretension that sets itself up against the knowledge of God, and we take captive every thought to make it obedient to Christ."

(II Corinthians 10:3-5)

Peg #15 is the 15 mile marker. Fifteen miles to Heaven, your final destination in Christ.

Peg #15

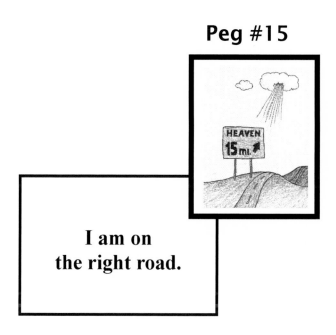

I am on
the right road.

"Enter through the narrow gate. For wide is the gate and broad is the road that leads to destruction, and many enter through it. But small is the gate and narrow the road that leads to life, and only a few find it." (Matthew 7:13-14)

The water ladle is peg #16. Salt makes you thirsty and water quenches your thirst. You are the salt of the earth, and you also have your spiritual thirst quenched by Christ.

Peg #16

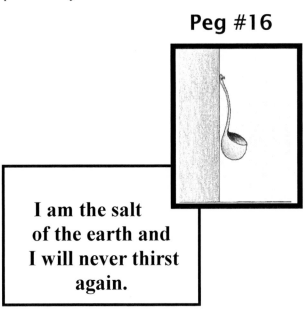

**I am the salt
of the earth and
I will never thirst
again.**

"You are the salt of the earth. But if the salt loses its saltiness, how can it be made salty again? It is no longer good for anything, except to be thrown out and trampled by men." (Matthew 5:13)

"Jesus answered and said to her, 'Whoever drinks of this water will thirst again, but whoever drinks of the water that I shall give him will never thirst. But the water that I shall give him will become in him a fountain of water springing up into everlasting life.'" (John 4:13-14) NKJV

Peg #17 is the pocket knife stuck in a tree. The Old Testament priest used a knife to kill the sacrificial lamb. You are now a priest, called by God to point others to Jesus, the final Sacrifice.

Peg #17

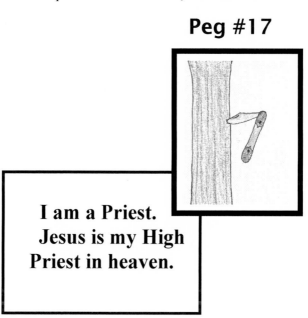

I am a Priest. Jesus is my High Priest in heaven.

"But you are a chosen people, a royal priesthood, a holy nation, a people belonging to God."
(I Peter 2:9a)

"The point of what we are saying is this: We do have such a high priest, who sat down at the right hand of the throne of the Majesty in heaven."
(Hebrews 8:1)

"Therefore he is able to save completely those who come to God through him, because he always lives to intercede for them." (Hebrews 7:25)

Peg #18 is the pair of eyeglasses. You have been given new spiritual eyes in Christ.

Peg #18

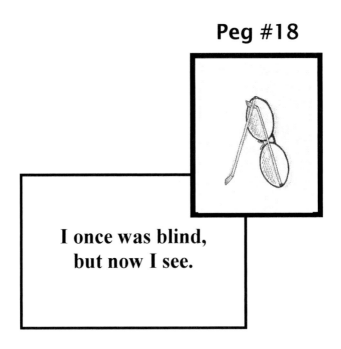

I once was blind, but now I see.

"He answered, '...one thing I know: that though I was blind, now I see.'" (John 9:25) NKJV

"And even if our gospel is veiled, it is veiled to those who are perishing. The god of this age has blinded the minds of unbelievers, so that they cannot see the light of the gospel of the glory of Christ, who is the image of God." (II Corinthians 4:3-4)

Peg #19 is the skinny girl holding a balloon on a string. The balloon is black, as a symbol of death. You are dead to sin, but alive to God.

Peg #19

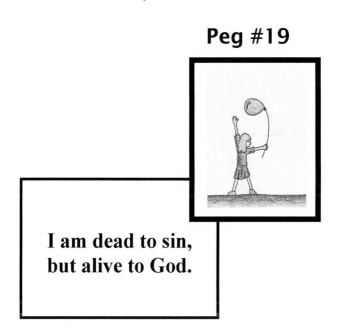

I am dead to sin, but alive to God.

"In the same way, count yourselves dead to sin but alive to God in Christ Jesus. Therefore do not let sin reign in your mortal body so that you obey its evil desires."   (Romans 6:11-12)

The coiled snake is peg #20. You can stomp on the snake, the devil, because the power of God in you is greater than the devil.

Peg #20

Greater is He who is in me than he who is in the world.

"You, dear children, are from God and have overcome them, because the One who is in you is greater than the one who is in the world."

(I John 4:4)

Peg #21 is "You must be 21 to enter." That doesn't apply to you, though, when it comes to Heaven. Your admission is guaranteed in Christ.

Peg #21

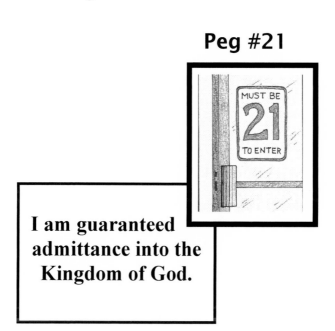

I am guaranteed admittance into the Kingdom of God.

"Now it is God who makes both us and you stand firm in Christ. He anointed us, set his seal of ownership on us, and put his Spirit in our hearts as a deposit, guaranteeing what is to come."
(II Corinthians 1:21-22)

Peg #22 is 22 sticks of dynamite bound together. A bunch of dynamite can blow up a hill or an old building, but see it here blowing up the devil and all evil.

Peg #22

Someday the devil and all evil will be destroyed.

"But the day of the Lord will come as a thief in the night, in which the heavens will pass away with a great noise, and the elements will melt with fervent heat; both the earth and the works that are in it will be burned up." (II Peter 3:10) NKJV

"The devil, who deceived them, was cast into the lake of fire and brimstone where the beast and the false prophet are. And they will be tormented day and night forever and ever." (Revelation 20:10) NKJV

Peg #23 is the number on the basketball uniform.
Just as the player who wore that uniform was an
ambassador for basketball, so you are an
ambassador for Christ.

Peg #23

**I am an ambassador
for Christ.**

"Now then, we are ambassadors for Christ,
as though God were pleading through us:
we implore you on Christ's behalf,
be reconciled to God."
 (II Corinthians 5:20) NKJV

Peg #24 is 24 bars of gold safely hidden in a safe,
just as your life is safely hidden with Christ in God.

Peg #24

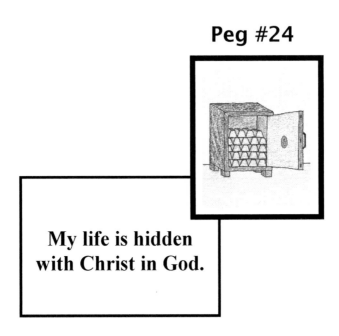

**My life is hidden
with Christ in God.**

"For you died, and your life is hidden with Christ in
God. When Christ, who is our life appears, then you
also will appear with Him in glory."
(Colossians 3:3-4) NKJV

The 25 cent piece is peg #25. Just as you need a 25 cent piece (or two) for *calling* someone on a payphone, so you have a great *calling*, the greatest calling in the world.

Peg #25

I have life's highest calling... serving the King of kings and Lord of lords.

"As a prisoner for the Lord, then, I urge you to live a life worthy of the calling you have received. Be completely humble and gentle; be patient, bearing with one another in love. Make every effort to keep the unity of the Spirit though the bond of peace." (Ephesians 4:1-3)

Peg #26 is an ice cream scoop, for dipping out some light, sweet ice cream, reminding you of your sweet future glory in Christ.

Peg #26

I consider that our present sufferings are not worth comparing with the (sweet) glory that will be revealed in us.

"For I consider that the sufferings of this present time are not worthy to be compared with the glory which shall be revealed in us." (Romans 8:18) NKJV

There you have it, the tools to memorize up to 105 glorious riches in Christ. And, oh, what marvelous riches we have been given, all by His grace. We should never ever doubt the great value placed upon us by our gracious God. Rejoice and give thanks, continually.

Is it any wonder Scripture so often says, remember, remember, remember, don't forget, don't forget, don't forget. We so *easily* get off focus. Our thinking becomes negative and unbiblical, and our lifestyles are *much* more cultural than Scriptural. As Peter says, we can get so off track that it's actually possible to "forget that we have been cleansed from our past sins" (II Peter 1:9). Amazing! Even as believers, if we are not focused on Christ and growing in our faith, we can live like pagans!

Way too often, we, as believers, can take God's grace and riches for granted. We are very blessed and sometimes very spoiled. If you can imagine Mephibosheth, going from "dead dog" to an heir of the king, then showing no gratitude to the king, or any respect or allegiance to the king, then that's a pretty good picture of many Christians today. "Hey, thanks for saving me, but don't ask me to make any changes or any sacrifices, or to leave my comfort zone."

As you truly think about your riches in Christ, may your life be transformed each and every day. And may the following fresh focus on the cross also help you stay focused on who you are and what you are in Christ.

"What if he did this to make the riches of his glory known to the objects of his mercy, whom he prepared in advance for glory?"

(Romans 9:23)

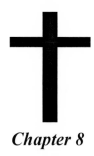

Chapter 8

Responding to the Riches - Five Focuses

Now, in the remaining chapters, I want to challenge you to *respond* to the riches you possess in Christ. Jesus would remind us, "For everyone to whom much is given, from him much will be required" (Luke 12:48b) NKJV. As a believer in Jesus Christ, you are immeasurably blessed and rich. You have eternal life. Nothing can separate you from His love. Heaven is your home. You are secure in Christ.

And also remember, you've been bought with a price, the blood of Christ. You are *owned* by God. So now it is time to understand and apply a proper and Biblical response to your spiritual wealth.

I personally find "visual reminders" to be extremely helpful. Properly used, they can help us stay focused on what's important in life, and prevent us from thinking, talking, and acting improperly.

In the Old Testament, God's people used unleavened bread and piles of stones as reminders.

In the New Testament, early Christians used "the sign of the fish" as a visual tool.

Today, bracelets, necklaces, and even bumper stickers are used by Christians (hopefully along with a consistent testimony and lifestyle) as reminders of our faith and Biblical truths.

The one visual that I'd like to focus on in this chapter is the cross. Each morning I like to draw a small cross on my finger, just below my wedding ring. It reminds me of five important truths, which I'll explain in the following pages. Let me encourage you, as you study these five exciting and helpful principles, to from this time forward, see the cross in a different light.

Hopefully it already reminds you of the One who lovingly and graciously died for you, and may you never be unmoved by that profound truth. Now let's add five new dimensions to the reminder of the cross. (By the way, see the cross also as a "t", as in truth, to help memorize these life-changing principles.)

Today is the day you have

"This is the day the LORD has made; we will rejoice and be glad in it" (Psalm 118:24) KJV.

"...but one thing I do: Forgetting what is behind and straining toward what is ahead, I press on toward the goal to win the prize for which God has called me heavenward in Christ Jesus" (Philippians 3:13b-14).

Today is the day you have. Yesterday is gone, and tomorrow is not guaranteed. You should learn from the past but not dwell on it. You should make goals and plans for the future, but prayerfully consult God and commit them all to Him, and remember that all of life is extremely fragile and tentative. Today is the day you have to serve God and make a difference in someone's life. Today. Today is your opportunity.

I once did a funeral service for a man in Michigan. After the service we all went to the man's house for a meal. As we stood around chatting and eating, I noticed a brand-new motor home in the driveway. I was told that the man who had died had made plans to take that brand-new motor home to Florida on that very day. So "today," instead of arriving in sunny Florida, he was instead experiencing the reality of eternity, while his house was filled with dozens of friends and relatives, eating ham sandwiches and potato salad in his honor. Today. Today is the day you have. Use it wisely.

"Now listen, you who say, 'Today or tomorrow we will go to this or that city, spend a year there, carry on business and make money.' Why, you do not even know what will happen tomorrow. What is your life? You are a mist that appears for a little while and then vanishes" (James 4:13-14).

†oday you must †ake up your cross

"Then he said to them all, 'If anyone desires to come after Me, let him deny himself, and take up his cross daily, and follow Me'" (Luke 9:23) NKJV.

I wear a cross around my neck. So does my wife. The church buildings where I've pastored are adorned with crosses. A lot of athletes have crosses as tattoos, and many rock singers wear huge ornate crosses. We sing a praise chorus at church that speaks of "the wonderful cross." But that is certainly the irony of the cross, for the cross historically was used for the purpose of torture and death.

If a person "took up his cross," it meant that he would soon suffer and die upon it, and crucifixion was a common and brutal form of torture and execution, perfected during the Roman Empire.

So consider again Jesus' "invitation." He said if anyone (no exceptions) would come after him, he *must* (absolutely required) deny himself, take up his cross daily, and follow Jesus. In other words, if we really are going to be followers of Jesus, we must daily die to ourselves - die to our selfish ambitions, die to our own agendas, die to our pride. Paul said, "I die every day" (I Corinthians 15:31a).

He also wrote, "I have been crucified with Christ and I no longer live, but Christ lives in me. The life I live in the body, I live by faith in the Son of God, who loved me and gave himself for me" (Galatians 2:20).

"Since, then, you have been raised with Christ, set your hearts on things above, where Christ is seated at the right hand of God. Set your minds on things above, not on earthly things. For you died, and your life is now hidden with Christ in God. When Christ, who is your life, appears, then you will also appear with him in glory" (Colossians 3:1-4).

"What shall we say, then? Shall we go on sinning so that grace may increase? By no means! We died to sin; how can we live in it any longer?" (Romans 6:1-2).

"Now if we died with Christ, we believe that we will also live with him. For we know that since Christ was raised from the dead, he cannot die again; death no longer has mastery over him. The death he died, he died to sin once for all; but the life he lives, he lives to God.

"In the same way, count yourselves dead to sin but alive to God in Christ Jesus. Therefore do not let sin reign in your mortal body so that you obey its evil desires" (Romans 6:8-12).

Get the picture? As followers of Christ, we've died with him, risen with him, and been raised to heaven with him. Although we still must live out our lives in this sinful, fallen world, we've been given a new standing in Christ, and the power of the Holy Spirit to live a life not of perpetual defeat, but of daily ongoing victory. So we don't have to give in to the same old sins and the same old habits.

Start living *today* in the power of Christ. Consider yourself "dead to sin, but alive to God" (Romans 6:11). "I can do all things through Christ who strengthens me" (Philippians 4:13) NKJV.

†oday you must give †hanks

I was driving to a lunch appointment one day, and while I was driving, I was having a party. Okay, it was a pity party, and I was the one and only guest. I was thinking about a number of frustrations in life, and I was becoming more bitter, cynical, and unhappy by the minute.

At the same time, right in the midst of my "party," I knew exactly what I needed to do. See I'd been down this path before, and it always led me to the same conclusion and necessary action. I needed to give thanks. Yes, essentially my problem was one of disobedience. I was disobeying a basic Scriptural command. I wasn't being thankful as I'm commanded to be. "Give thanks in all circumstances, for this is God's will for you in Christ Jesus" (I Thessalonians 5:18).

Although I knew what I needed to do, I also knew it would be the end of the "party". See, sometimes we like to wallow in self-pity, even though we are miserable in the midst of it. So my thought was, "all right, all right, I'll do it. And I know what will happen." And sure enough, it did.

As I began to thank God for health and material blessings, past acts of God's mercy, and my spiritual riches, my attitude changed. Then I confessed my unthankfulness, thanked God for His forgiveness, and then even thanked Him for the frustrations I was going through. As I arrived at my lunch appointment, I was a man with a "transformed mind" (Romans 12:2). I was able to care about, and minister to, the man I was having lunch with, whereas an hour ago I would have been totally self-absorbed. I'm convinced that "giving thanks" is a tremendously important key to a successful Christian life.

Whenever we're negative, complaining, or unthankful, we're living in disobedience to a clear Scriptural command. Rising above our circumstances, and how we feel, to be obedient to God, brings honor to Him and blessing to us.

But isn't it hypocritical to give thanks when you really don't feel like it? Not really. If we only honored obedience to what we "feel like," we might not go to work or even get up in the morning. "Give thanks in all circumstances, for this is God's will for you in Christ Jesus" (I Thessalonians 5:18).

Looking for God's will? Look no further. Scripture is clear. Start giving thanks. In all circumstances. God always honors and blesses obedience to His Word and will.

Today you must watch your Tongue

"Do not let any unwholesome talk come out of your mouths, but only what is helpful for building others up according to their needs, that it may benefit those who listen" (Ephesians 4:29).

I once shared an object lesson with a group of Vacation Bible School kids entitled, "The World's Most Dangerous Weapon." They learned that it was not a gun or a knife or a bomb, but the "world's most dangerous weapon," that I had concealed in a paper bag, was a tongue (cow tongue for illustration's sake).

More people have been hurt and destroyed by hurtful words than by any other weapon. Families are divided, children are crushed, spouses are devastated, churches are destroyed, friends are alienated, and war and hostilities are fueled by careless and dangerous words. "The tongue has the power of life and death" (Proverbs 18:21a).

"When words are many, sin is not absent, but he who holds his tongue is wise" (Proverbs 10:19).

"Reckless words pierce like a sword, but the tongue of the wise brings healing" (Proverbs 12:18).

"He who guards his mouth and his tongue keeps himself from calamity" (Proverbs 21:23).

We know that "no man can tame the tongue" (James 3:8) NKJV, but Scripture is abundantly clear over and over again that we are responsible for our words.

"But I tell you that men will have to give account on the day of judgment for every careless word they have spoken. For by your words you will be acquitted, and by your words you will be condemned" (Matthew 12:36-37).

Sobering warnings. By God's grace, let's *weigh* our words and seek His help to *guide* our words. May we *think* before we speak, and always consider the potential impact of our words. May we pray like David, "Set a guard, O LORD, over my mouth; keep watch over the door of my lips" (Psalm 141:3) NKJV. "He who would love life and see good days, let him refrain his tongue from evil, and his lips from speaking deceit" (I Peter 3:10) NKJV.

Watch your words. Weigh them. They can edify, empower, and encourage, or they can injure, devastate, and destroy.

✝oday you must ✝ransfer your stock

"Casting all your care on him because he cares for you" (I Peter 5:7) NKJV.

"Trust in the Lord with all your heart and lean not on your own understanding; in all your ways acknowledge Him, and He shall direct your paths" (Proverbs 3:5-6) NKJV.

"It is better to trust in the LORD than to put confidence in man" (Psalm 118:8) NKJV.

I've heard that the above verse is the middle verse in the Bible. I'll admit though, that I haven't gone forward and backward through all of Scripture to verify that.

I do understand, however, that a Scriptural principle shines through that verse and many others like it. The principle urges us to "put all our stock in God, and God alone."

God alone is completely faithful and trustworthy. God alone will never fail. God alone is worthy of our praise. Don't put others on a pedestal. Don't lay unreal or unfair expectations on yourself or others. Admit your utter dependence upon God. He alone gives to all men "life and breath and everything else" (Acts 17:25).

Don't put unrealistic stock in *yourself* or your *own* abilities. Put all your trust in God and *His* power. You and I are fickle, unstable, unpredictable, and flawed, due to our sin.

The only good in any of us is from God and His grace. "I know that nothing good lives in me, that is, in my sinful nature (my flesh)" (Romans 7:18a).

So transfer all your stock into a God who can do anything, and who can do great things *through* you because of who He is. Step out in great faith and expectation today, knowing that "God's grace will be sufficient for you" (II Corinthians 12:9).

✝ **Live *today* with excitement and anticipation.**

✝ ***Today* is what you have.**

✝ **Take up your cross *today*.**

✝ **Give thanks *today*.**

✝ **Watch your tongue *today*.**

✝ **Transfer your stock *today*.**

✝ **Rejoice and utilize your riches *today*.**

"Humility and the fear
of the LORD bring
wealth and honor
and life".

(Proverbs 22:4)

Chapter 9

Responding to the Riches - Raising Your Gaze

I was out in my backyard one summer afternoon when the local game warden stopped by. He also attended the church where I pastored, so we had a lot of good discussions about hunting, fishing, and any number of spiritual things.

As we were chatting on this particular day, suddenly he looked up and said, "Wow, look at that helicopter!"

I squinted into the bright sky and responded, "I don't see a helicopter. All I see are a few turkey buzzards circling around."

"No, higher," he said, and sure enough, as I raised my gaze, there was a life flight helicopter circling in the clear blue sky.

Yes, I needed to raise my gaze. I needed to lift my focus. I needed to elevate my eyesight to get it off the turkey buzzards, and onto the helicopter that my friend was trying to point out to me.

So it is with life. A lot of us need to "raise our gaze." Too often as Christians we are negative, pessimistic complainers. As someone once said, "we look like we've been baptized in vinegar and weaned on a dill pickle," and we act and talk as if we're carrying the weight of the world on our shoulders, instead of rejoicing in our present blessings and our glorious eternal destiny.

Look, we certainly can't control all our circumstances, but we *can* control and elevate our attitudes. And we do that by what we *focus* on, and what we *meditate* on.

"Finally, brethren, whatever things are true, whatever things are honest, whatever things are just, whatever things are pure, whatever things are lovely, whatever things are of good report; if there be any virtue, and if any praise, think on these things" (Philippians 4:8) KJV.

How else could Paul go on to say, "I have learned to be content whatever the circumstances" (Philippians 4:11)? It was because of his *focus*, what he chose to dwell on, to meditate on.

If you're familiar with Paul's writings, you know that his life was not an easy, carefree one. In fact, it was anything but that. It was full of persecution and trials, but Paul's mindset was the following:

"I consider that our present sufferings are not worth comparing with the glory that will be revealed in us" (Romans 8:18).

"Therefore we do not lose heart. Though outwardly we are wasting away, yet inwardly we are being renewed day by day. For our light and momentary troubles are achieving for us an eternal glory that far outweighs them all. So we fix our eyes not on what is seen, but on what is unseen. For what is seen is temporary, but what is unseen is eternal" (II Corinthians 4: 16-18).

Yes, as the old saying goes, attitude does

determine altitude—how high we fly or how low we wallow. Let me illustrate that with one more little story.

I was out deer hunting one time with my bow. (Now if you're concerned with the fact that I was hunting those "poor little deer," understand that deer are in much more danger of dying from high cholesterol or old age than from my bow hunting ability). But as I was sitting there quietly in the woods, I realized that I could look at my time there in one of two ways.

First, I could see it as a no-win situation. "Oh, man, if I get a deer, I have to go to all the trouble of dressing it out, processing it, etc., etc. And if I don't get one, I've wasted all this time. Either way, I lose!"

Or, I could look at it as a no-lose situation. "Wow, if I get a deer, great! That's why I'm out here. But if I don't, that's great too. I won't have to mess with it. And besides, what a beautiful, quiet time to pray, meditate, and enjoy nature. Either way, I win!" It's exactly the same situation, but with completely different attitudes.

And so it is, again with life. We can choose to approach life with faith, hope, joy, and optimism, or with a pessimistic, judgmental, negative, complaining spirit. No, you can't choose all your circumstances, but you *can* choose your attitude.

A very negative young lady once asked me, "Why do you always have to see the good in everything?" Well, I don't, really. But I believe we're supposed to. As Christians, with all we have in Christ, and who we are in Christ, to not see the good would indeed be a sin and a shame.

Like Mephibosheth, we've been graciously promoted from "dead dog" status to guests (and sons and daughters) at the King's table. And no matter what else life throws at us, we will forever dine at that table. So rejoice!

"Rejoice in the Lord
always.
And again I say
rejoice!"

(Philippians 4:4)

"I know your
afflictions and your
poverty – yet you
are rich!"

(Revelation 2:9a)

Chapter 10

God is Looking for a Few Good Men and Women

I believe that we, as Christians living in America, are very blessed and very spoiled. We really truly have no idea of how good we have it.

Let me just challenge you, with whatever time God blesses you on this earth, to rise above, by God's grace, all the petty, trivial, materialistic, self-centered attitude and lifestyle that sadly characterizes so much of Christianity and "Churchianity" in America today.

May we all be challenged, in response to God's riches, by the following words of an unknown author, who shortly after writing them was martyred for his faith. May his powerful words and focus be our own, and may we be faithful until we see Jesus face to face.

I am a Soldier in the Army of My God

"I am a soldier in the army of my God.
The Lord Jesus Christ is my commanding officer.
The Holy Bible is my code of conduct.
Faith, prayer, and the Word
are my weapons of warfare.
I have been taught by the Holy Spirit, trained by
experience, tried by adversity and tested by fire.
I am a volunteer in this army, and I am enlisted for
eternity. I will either retire in this army at the rapture
or die in this army; but I will not get out, sell out, be
talked out, or be pushed out.
I am faithful, reliable, capable, and dependable.
If my God needs me, I am there.
If He needs me to teach the children, work with the
youth, help adults or just sit and learn,
He can use me because I am there!
I am a soldier.
I am not a baby.
I do not need to be pampered, petted, primed up,
pumped up, picked up or pepped up.
I am a soldier.
No one has to call me, remind me, write me,
visit me, entice me, or lure me.
I am a soldier.
I am not a wimp.
I am in place, saluting my King, obeying His orders,
praising His name, and building His kingdom!
No one has to send me flowers, gifts, food, cards,
candy or give me handouts.
I do not need to be cuddled, cradled,
cared for or catered to.
I am committed.

I cannot have my feelings hurt
bad enough to turn me around.
I cannot be discouraged enough to turn me aside.
I cannot lose enough to cause me to quit.
When Jesus called me into His army, I had nothing.
If I end up with nothing, I will still come out ahead.
I will win.
My God has, and will continue to
supply all of my needs.
I am more than a conqueror.
I will always triumph.
I can do all things through Christ.
Devils cannot defeat me.
People cannot disillusion me.
Weather cannot weary me.
Sickness cannot stop me.
Battles cannot beat me.
Money cannot buy me.
Governments cannot silence me
and hell cannot handle me.
I am a soldier.
Even death cannot destroy me.
For when my Commander calls me
from this battlefield,
He will promote me to allow me to live with Him.
I am a soldier in the army,
and I'm marching claiming victory.
I will not give up.
I will not turn around.
I am a soldier, marching heaven bound."

**"Endure hardship with us
like a good soldier of Christ Jesus."
(II Timothy 2:3)**

"You will be made rich in every way so that you can be generous on every occasion, and through us your generosity will result in thanksgiving to God."

(II Corinthians 9:11)

Chapter 11

Responding to the Riches -
Joyously Sharing the Wealth

Yes, if you truly know Jesus Christ, you are eternally rich in Him. Like the orphaned Mephibosheth, you have gone from "dead dog" status to a child of the King.

You have come from the land of Lo Debar, which means "No Pasture" (II Samuel 9:5), to a land of *rich* pasture, dining at the table of the King of all kings.

As Mephibosheth was shown favor for Jonathan's sake, so you will eternally be shown favor for Jesus' sake.

Now it is time to share the wealth. Those who are blessed are to be a blessing, understanding our richness in Christ should in no way produce complacency or mediocrity, but a passion to share with others what we have discovered and received, the incomparable riches of Jesus Christ.

Back during the days of Elisha the prophet, the land of Samaria was under siege by the King of Aram and his mighty army (II Kings 6-7). In the midst of a terrible famine caused by the siege, four men devised a risky plan.

"Now there were four leprous men at the entrance of the gate; and they said to one another, 'why are we sitting here until we die? If we say, "We will enter the city," the famine is in the city, and we shall die there. And if we sit here, we die also. Now therefore, come, let us surrender to the army of the Syrians. If they keep us alive, we shall live; and if they kill us, we shall only die.'

"And they rose at twilight to go to the camp of the Syrians: and when they had come to the outskirts of the Syrian camp, to their surprise no one was there. For the LORD had caused the army of the Syrians to hear the noise of chariots and the noise of horses - the noise of a great army; so they said to one another, 'Look, the king of Israel has hired against us the kings of the Hittites and the kings of the Egyptians to attack us!'

"Therefore they arose and fled at twilight, and left the camp intact - their tents, their horses, and their donkeys - and they fled for their lives. And when these lepers came to the outskirts of the camp, they went into one tent and ate and drank, and carried from it silver and gold and clothing, and went and hid them; then they came back and entered another tent, and carried some from there also, and went and hid it.

"Then they said to one another, 'We are not doing right. This day is a day of good news, and we remain silent'" (II Kings 7:3-9a) NKJV.

Thankfully, the lepers recognized their self-absorbed greediness, and began to share their incredible newfound wealth. So now let me remind you and challenge you with this:

Much greater than the lepers with their newfound riches, much greater than Mephibosheth living like a prince in King David's palace, so we are spiritually rich in Christ, now and for eternity.

So certainly, in view of being so very blessed, so very rich, so very favored by God's grace, may we generously and continuously give fully of ourselves and all we are, and all we have, to bring others to richness in Christ and to further the Kingdom of God. May the passion of each truly saved and rescued child of God be to bring as many to God's table as we possibly can.

Remember this: The world is sick with sin, but you have the cure. The world is getting more rotten all the time, but you are the salt of the earth. The world is full of darkness, but you are the light of the world. The world apart from Christ is dwelling in death, but you know the One who conquered the grave. The world is full of questions. You know the Answer.

Epilogue

You will find on the following pages, two lists of spiritual riches in Christ. The first list contains many of the alphabetical riches listed on pages 25-56, and most of the riches which can be memorized using the memory pegs. I have seen some people memorize this list of 57 riches in an hour or two, using the tools provided in this book.

My youngest son is eleven years old, and he's been reciting the list of 57 riches to himself before he goes to sleep at night.

A former missionary pilot shared the riches with his young daughter, who hadn't been sleeping through the night. As she memorized them, the good night's rest for her (and dad and mom) became a reality.

I know of a lady who quotes the riches on her morning prayer walk, and she shares how God's peace flows over her as she's reminded of who she is and what she is in Christ.

A group of young adults from our church recently went to Maui, Hawaii to share the Gospel and the 57 riches with over eighty children in grades two through eight at a camp in the West Maui Mountains. First, the camp staff memorized the riches, and then many of the kids memorized them as well. It brought tears to my eyes to hear of one young girl joyfully running out of the longhouse, having just recited the riches, shouting, "I'm rich in Christ. All my sins are forgiven!"

The second list contains 105 riches. This expanded list includes all the riches found in the first list, plus the rest of the alphabetical riches and the rest of the riches which can be hung on the memory pegs. Memorization of this list is also very achievable by using the tools in this book. You may even think of more riches to add to your list through your own study of the Scriptures. Each morning as I drive to work, I like to recite, out loud, the 105 riches I possess in Christ (plus a couple more I've discovered). It takes less than five minutes, but it always helps transform and mold my thinking for the day.

Let me encourage you to memorize and meditate on the great riches you possess in Christ, given to you by His grace. Your thinking will be transformed, and your life will be changed.

See yourself, blessed like Mephibosheth, and be filled with eternal gratitude. Then go boldly into your world and make a difference. Love and serve God and others. Be a shining light in an increasingly dark world. God wants to use you in a mighty way in these last days. Help enable others to joyfully say, "I'm rich in Christ. All my sins are forgiven!"

God bless you as you rejoice in your unchangeable, irrefutable, undeniable riches in Christ, and as you point others to Jesus, the only Hope of the world.

> "Jesus said..., 'I am the way and the truth and the life. No one comes to the Father except through Me.'" (John 14:6) NKJV

"You will keep in perfect peace him whose mind is steadfast, because he trusts in you. Trust in the LORD forever, for the LORD, the LORD, is the rock eternal." (Isaiah 26:3-4)

"Your word I have hidden in my heart, that I might not sin against you."

(Psalms 119:11) NKJV

57
Unchangeable, Irrefutable, Undeniable Riches In Christ

1. **All** my sins are forgiven.
2. I am **bought** with a price, the **blood** of Christ.
3. I am **complete** in Christ.
4. I am **delivered** from the **dominion** of **darkness.**
5. I have **eternal** life.
6. God is my **faithful Father**.
7. I have been **given** the **gift** of **grace**.
8. **Heaven** is my **home**.
9. With God nothing is **impossible.**
10. **Jesus** is my best friend.
11. I am a child of the **King**.
12. Nothing can separate me from God's **love**.
13. I am **made** in the image of God.
14. **Never, never, never**, will God leave me or forsake me.
15. God **owns** me
16. I have **peace** with God.
17. My life has great **quality.**
18. I've been **redeemed** by the blood of the Lamb.
19. I am **secure** in Christ.
20. I've come to know the **truth** and the **truth** has set me free.
21. God loves me with an **unconditional** love.
22. I have great **value** in Christ.
23. I have great **victory** in Christ.
24. I have great **wisdom** in Christ.
25. I have an **excellent** life.
26. I am **yoked** together with Christ.
27. I have great **zeal** for God.

28. My name is written in the Book of Life.
29. I am clothed with the righteousness of God.
30. I am a child of God.
31. I am an heir of God.
32. I am a saint.
33. I am rich in Christ.
34. I am a new creature in Christ.
35. I've been given great power from on high.
36. All things work together for good to those that love God.
37. I am no longer in darkness, but I am in the light.
38. I follow Jesus, the light of the world.
39. I am called to be the light of the world.
40. I am chosen by God.
41. I am justified.
42. I am accepted in the Beloved.
43. I am holy.
44. I am more than a conqueror.
45. I have divine power to demolish strongholds.
46. I am on the right road.
47. I am the salt of the earth.
48. I will never thirst again.
49. I am a priest.
50. I once was blind, but now I see.
51. I am dead to sin, but alive to God.
52. Greater is He who is in me, than he who is in the world.
53. I am guaranteed admittance into the Kingdom of God.
54. Someday the devil and all evil will be destroyed.
55. I am an ambassador for Christ.
56. My life is hidden with Christ in God.
57. I have life's highest calling – serving the King of kings and Lord of lords.

105
Unchangeable, Irrefutable, Undeniable Riches In Christ (Expanded List)

1. **All** my sins are forgiven.
2. I can do **all** things through Christ who strengthens me.
3. God is **able** to save me completely.
4. I am **bought** with a price, the **blood** of Christ.
5. I am **born** from above.
6. I will have a **brand**-new **body**.
7. I am complete in **Christ**.
8. I am **created** in Christ to do good works.
9. I can **cast** all of my **cares** upon Him, because He **cares** for me.
10. I am **delivered** from the **dominion** of **darkness.**
11. I have **direct** access into the presence of God.
12. I have **eternal** life.
13. As far as the **east** is from the west, so has God taken my sins from me.
14. God is my **faithful Father**.
15. I am **free** in Christ.
16. I have been **given** the **gift** of **grace**.
17. Every day is a **gift** from God.
18. **Heaven** is my **home**.
19. My **hope** is an anchor.
20. The **Holy** Spirit is in me.
21. With God nothing is **impossible.**
22. God's gifts are **irrevocable**.
23. **Jesus** is my best friend.
24. **Jesus** is my Savior.

25. **Jesus** is my Lord.
26. **Jesus** is coming back soon for me.
27. I am a child of the **King**.
28. I **know** I have eternal life.
29. I **know** God.
30. God **knows** me.
31. Nothing can separate me from God's **love**.
32. Because He **lives**, I too shall **live**.
33. I am **made** in the image of God.
34. I have received God's **mercy**.
35. I have the **mind** of Christ.
36. **Never, never, never** will God leave or forsake me.
37. My sins are **nailed** to the cross.
38. God will meet all my **needs**.
39. God **owns** me.
40. I can **open** my mouth wide and God will fill it.
41. I am an **overcomer.**
42. I have **peace** with God.
43. I am **perfect** in His sight.
44. My life has great **purpose.**
45. My life has great **quality**.
46. I've been **redeemed** by the blood of the lamb.
47. I am **raised** with Christ.
48. God is my **refuge** and strength.
49. I am **secure** in Christ.
50. I am **sealed** by the Holy **Spirit**.
51. I am **saved.**
52. I am **seated** in the heavenlies.
53. The Lord is my **shepherd**.
54. I am **sanctified.**
55. I've come to know the **truth** and the **truth** has set me free.
56. I can **trust** in the LORD with all my heart.
57. God loves me with an **unconditional** love.
58. God loves me with an **unfailing** love.

59. I have great **value** in Christ..
60. I have great **victory** in Christ.
61. I have great **wisdom** in Christ.
62. I can **worship** the Father in spirit and truth.
63. I am God's **workmanship**.
64. I am a **witness** for God.
65. I have an **excellent** life.
66. I am **yoked** together with Christ.
67. Jesus Christ is the same **yesterday,** today, and forever.
68. I have great **zeal** for God.
69. I have come to Mt. **Zion**.
70. My name is written in the Book of Life.
71. I am clothed with the righteousness of God.
72. I am a child of God.
73. I am an heir of God.
74. I am a saint.
75 I am rich is Christ.
76. I am a new creature in Christ.
77. God will complete His work in me.
78. I've been given great power from on high.
79. All things work together for good to those that love God.
80. God makes all things beautiful in His time.
81. I am no longer in darkness, but I am in the light.
82. I follow Jesus, the light of the world.
83. I am called to be the light of the world.
84. I am chosen by God.
85. I am adopted by God.
86. I am no longer condemned.
87. I am justified.
88. I am accepted in the Beloved.
89. I am holy.
90. I am more than a conqueror.
91. I have divine power to demolish strongholds.

92. I am on the right road.
93. I am the salt of the earth.
94 I will never thirst again.
95. I am a priest.
96. Jesus is my High Priest in Heaven.
97. I once was blind, but now I see.
98. I am dead to sin, but alive to God.
99. Greater is He who is in me than he who is in the world.
100. I am guaranteed admittance into the Kingdom of God.
101. Someday the devil and all evil will be destroyed.
102. I am an ambassador for Christ.
103. My life is hidden with Christ in God.
104. I have life's highest calling—serving the King of kings and Lord of lords.
105. I consider that our present sufferings are not worth comparing with the (sweet) glory that will be revealed in us.

An Invitation to Dine

If you have truly committed your life to Jesus Christ, trusting Him alone to cleanse you of your sins, and confessing Him as your Lord and risen Savior, then you already have a place reserved for you at the King's table. If you are not certain of your eternal destiny and your status with God, realize today that God loves you and He sent His Son to die for *you*, for *your* sins, and offers you today the opportunity to be saved, and to dine with Him at His glorious table for all eternity.

"Here I am! I stand at the door and knock. If anyone hears my voice and opens the door, I will come in and eat with him, and he with me." (Revelation 3:20)

"That if you confess with your mouth, 'Jesus is Lord,' and believe in your heart that God raised him from the dead, you will be saved. For it is with your heart that you believe and are justified, and it is with your mouth that you confess and are saved." (Romans 10:9-10)

Prayer of Salvation:
Dear Lord,

Thank you for the gift of eternal life. I admit that I am a sinner and that I cannot save myself. I believe Jesus is the Son of God and that He died for my sins and rose again from the dead. I now put my complete trust in Jesus Christ alone for my salvation and eternal life. Thank you for saving me. Help me now to turn away from sin, and live for you.

In Jesus' name, Amen.

"My purpose is that they may be encouraged in heart and united in love, so that they may have the full riches of complete understanding, in order that they may know the mystery of God, namely, Christ, in whom are hidden all the treasures of wisdom and knowledge."

(Colossians 2:2-3)

Interested in an unforgettable
<u>King's Table Seminar</u>
for your Church,
Christian School
or Group Gathering?
Or need more copies of
Rich in Christ?

Write to:

Jack Teeple
208 S. Main
Hicksville, OH 43526.

Or

Email Address:
RichinChrist@gmail.com

Website:
RICHINCHRIST.COM